Class

wealth and power
in neoliberal Britain

Lindsey German

COUNTERFIRE

Contents

Introduction

The terms Thatcherism and Blairism have entered into international political language. British politics for over 30 years has been characterised by the continuing assault on working-class organisation, the destruction of many public services, deregulation and internationalisation of capital, the spreading of an ideology of individual advance over collectivity and co-operation, a widening and unconscionable gap between rich and poor, and an aggressive and rampant imperialism and militarism.

If Margaret Thatcher was the ideological Tory, determined to revenge the defeats inflicted on her party and more widely on her class by a militant working-class in the 1960s and 1970s, Tony Blair was her ambitious apprentice. He was determined to take one of the largest working-class parties in Europe towards the centre ground, triangulating a politics which stood for an abandonment of the old post-war consensus of a mixed economy, full employment and a welfare state. Central to these projects' success was the systematic weakening of a working-class movement which had emerged from the Second World War organisationally strong, and which by the late 1960s was demonstrating a militancy with which it had not always been associated. In response to an employers' offensive which was trying to hold down wages and increase productivity, workers fought back.

By the early 1970s strikes were referred to internationally as the 'British disease'. In Europe, only Italy was comparable in terms of the frequency and scale of industrial action. This action was often led by young, militant workers in industries such as the automobile industry. Influenced by some of the more liberal and radical ideas of the 1960s, they were products of an era of full employment, rising wages, an expanding welfare state and an increase in education. They developed the confidence to take on the employers.

They were from a generation which experienced a real rise in both actual wages and the social wage, bringing wider improvements in their living standards. They were not prepared to see a reversal of that situation. Groups such as the coal miners, who had not seen national industrial action since the 1920s, showed a new militancy, as did many groups of predominantly women workers, including teachers and health workers, who campaigned against low pay.[1]

It would be hard to recognise this working-class in 21st century Britain. Inequality has grown to record levels, as the wealthy seize ever greater shares of wealth at the expense of the working-class and the poor. This is of course an international phenomenon in the age of neoliberalism. But the UK has in many ways worsened more than most relative to its traditions of welfare, high wages and strong working-class organisation.

Since the dual attacks of Thatcherism and Blairism, Britain has been associated with worsening living standards, an economy where manufacturing has deliberately been destroyed in favour of finance, speculative and housing bubbles, privatisation and deregulation, a race to the bottom in terms of wages and conditions, and a lowering of productivity as a result of falling levels of investment.

The capitalist class has benefited from more than three decades in which successive governments have given free rein to employers to implement a set of employment relations which have increased the rate of exploitation and worsened the conditions of millions of working-class people. One academic referred to the Bleak House of British employment relations over 20 years ago; today the term could be applied to much of the condition of the working-class in Britain today.[1]

Over a period of more than 30 years the traditional working-class trade-union organisations have declined by around half, from nearly 14 million in 1979 to below seven million now. Whereas then they represented nearly half the workforce, the proportion in trade-unions now is less than a quarter, and far lower even than that in private industry.[2] The traditional party of the trade-unions, Labour, has held office for 13 of those years but failed to reverse the attacks on working people, or to repeal laws which have made British unions the most constrained in Europe. In addition, it alienated many traditional supporters over issues ranging from privatisation to the series of wars in which it so enthusiastically joined.

The ideological onslaught on working-class people which has accompanied this relentless attack on their living standards has been considerable. While in Britain it has still not been the case, as it often seems to be in the US, that the working-class has been magically transmuted and 'disappeared' into a middle class and an underclass, elements of that process are in play. Sections of the working-class are demonized. Those reliant on state benefits have undergone two decades of attack and vilification which has been successful in two areas. It has forced the level of benefits for most recipients other than pensioners down in real terms, (and even UK pensioners are among the poorest in the developed world), and it has created a hostility, fuelled by the media and successive governments, towards recipients of benefits, denounced as scroungers and shirkers, considered by many as a new 'underclass', totally divorced from the 'respectable' working-class of old.

Television programmes watched by millions regularly portray such an underclass as feckless, scheming, lazy and worthless, and this is a picture echoed in the right-wing print media, with its seemingly endless diet of scare stories. A recent BBC radio programme charted this change of attitude, showing a series of portrayals of working-class life from the 1950s and 1960s as representing an affectionate portrayal of working-class people as serious, dignified and striving for better lives, and compared this to the almost totally derogatory portrayal now shown. This onslaught, repeated in the whole mainstream media, is readily seized on by politicians of all main parties.

I will argue here that although the above presents an accurate enough picture of the balance of class forces at present, and although the consciousness and organisation of the working-class has suffered a serious number of blows since the 1970s, it only tells part of the story. There are reasons for greater optimism about the future than this picture might suggest. Class organisations remain centrally important, with a degree of strengths in certain areas. This is true of the trade-unions, but also of Labour itself, which retains the electoral allegiance of millions of working-class people (nine million at the 2015 general election) in any contest with the right-wing and openly ruling-class party, the Conservatives.

Class consciousness is of course a different matter, but nonetheless there are signs of a growth in militant class consciousness, sometimes among groups who might hitherto not have identified as such. Changes in consciousness, even if they present significant barriers to organisation, should not in any case be confused with changes in class composition. The working-class has been through a period of profound change and re-composition, but it still exists as an exploited class, selling its labour power on a daily basis in order to earn its means of subsistence.

Indeed, I would argue that the working-class today has become more all-encompassing, has drawn in more elements of society, has seen its family under strain as all of its members are forced into wage labour on an increasing scale, and is larger and more diverse, and more subject to direct exploitation (especially in the case of women) than ever before. I will consider below the nature of the working-class, and whether its essentials remain despite the many fundamental changes which it has seen in its recent history.

It is also important to note that in addition to this there have been some remarkable leaps in consciousness among British working people. It would of course be a major error to ignore the low level of workplace combativity of the organised working-class. It would however be equally wrong to ignore others forms of expression of consciousness.

Since the turn of the 21st century there have been successive waves of protest on a range of different issues: the NHS, war and Palestine, students, refugees, housing, austerity generally, the role of the banks. There have been strikes by junior doctors, teachers, cleaners, transport workers, construction workers, nurses, university lecturers. There have been demonstrations, direct action, protests and Occupy. Even the vindication of the families who lost loved ones in the Hillsborough football disaster turned into a mass demonstration in criticism of the police, the media, the establishment and successive governments' failure to act.

We should not see these phenomena as separate from working-class organisation, but rather as at least some of the forms that present and future protest will take. If this is so, what implications does it have for the strengthening of class organisation and consciousness, and how do they relate to more traditional forms of organisation?

Finally, it would be impossible to write about class and organisation today without referring to the very significant upheavals inside the Labour Party in the past year, with the resounding victory of its most left-wing MP as leader of the party and therefore leader of what is known as 'Her Majesty's Opposition'. This is a phenomenon which it is fair to say took all those on the British left by surprise.

It is now well documented that Jeremy Corbyn, a veteran left-Labour MP, close ally of the former Labour minister Tony Benn, and campaigners around dozens of issues including a very large number of international and anti-imperialist campaigns, only stood as the result of a discussion among the small and isolated sections of the Labour left, where some argued that it was too weak to stand any candidate at all and that doing so would only reveal its weakness. Others, both in and outside Labour, argued that failing to do so would lead to a much more right-wing campaign which would not represent the true feelings of many Labour voters. This latter argument prevailed and Jeremy Corbyn was put forward, although he conceded that he might not receive enough nominations to even get into the contest.

However, it was obvious that Labour's defeat in May at the hands of the Tories (unexpected by most of its supporters) had led not just to demoralisation but to a wave of anger and militancy especially among young people who found the prospect of five years of majority Tory rule abhorrent. There were a number of demonstrations in various cities which took place in the days and weeks after the election, composed of large numbers of young people. A mass demonstration against austerity in late June 2015 attracted up to 250,000 people, and Corbyn found himself a keynote speaker.[4]

It was mostly the younger people around him who worked to win sufficient nominations from other MPs, to organise meetings and rallies for him and to argue against the scepticism of more experienced socialists that he had no possibility of winning. At the first televised debate with the other candidates, (one a hardline Blairite, the other two former ministers in Blair's and Brown's government who assumed that the campaign would be the usual pro-business, middle-of-the-road approach, accepting privatisation, cuts and austerity along with the whole neoliberal package) it became clear that Corbyn was receiving more support and developing a greater rapport with audiences than had previously been expected.

Despite the best efforts of the media and the

established figures within Labour, Corbyn swept to victory after a summer of mass rallies and a mass increase in Labour membership, including for the first time a supporters' category. The shock fallout of this result, when Corbyn scored more than his three rivals put together and the Blairite candidate scored less than 5%, is still reverberating through British politics.

While this is not the place to devote to a long analysis about Labour and Corbyn, it is important to recognise both the significance of the vote and the very deep contradictions revealed by it inside the Labour Party. Labour is historically the party closely identified with the organised working-class, through its connection with the trade-unions. It has achieved office on a number of occasions in the 20th and 21st centuries but has suffered a long-term decline in its support, and more recently an erosion of its base in the era of neoliberalism, a feature shared by the reformist parties internationally. It remains, however, an extremely strong organisation, not least because of its trade-union connection.

Traditionally, Labour has attracted left

activists to the party but its central structures have not reflected this. The right of the party has tended to dominate the PLP and the trade-union bureaucracy. Even today, the majority of MPs are not on the left, and far fewer Labour MPs voted for Corbyn than nominated him. He has faced a vicious and unprincipled onslaught from sections of his own MPs, from the media including the BBC and from very large sections of the British establishment. The Blairites are isolated within the party overall but still have influence in the apparatus and in parliament, as well as with a compliant media.

Yet Corbyn has created a huge opportunity of the left, as the most left-wing leader ever for Labour, and one who certainly stands a chance of becoming prime minister. But the nature of the Labour Party has not fundamentally changed. It remains a reformist party and of course an imperialist party which means that its right wing will always champion issues such as nuclear weapons, support for wars and for Israel. So despite the rise in Labour Party membership and support for Corbyn, there is a constant fight between right and left within the party.

Notes

1. For background to this see P Whitehead, *The Writing on the Wall*, (1985); C Harman, *The Fire Last Time*, (1988).

2. K Sisson, 'In search of HRM', *British Journal of Industrial Relations* 31, 2, (1993), pp.201-210.

3. Trade-union Statistics 2015 https://www.gov.uk/government/statistics/trade-union-statistics-2015 (accessed 19.6.16)

4. On the campaign, see for example A Snowdon, http://www.counterfire.org/articles/analysis/17968-the-end-of-blairism-jeremy-corbyn-the-labour-party-and-the-left (Accessed 19.6.16)

Class: some conceptions

In discussing class and organisation in Britain today, we need to develop an understanding of what we consider the working-class: does it still exist and if so where is it located? In order to consider this question, it is important to develop an analysis of what class is, and especially to look at how its composition has changed.

The existence of class as a concept dates only from the period of the Industrial Revolution, and all too often, popular conceptions of class tend to conjure up images of the industrial working-class which developed as result of that revolution and its aftermath. In Britain there is still a strong identification of class with a manual working-class, engaged in work in factories, shipyards and mines, these workforces and their unions dominated by men.

Seeing the working-class purely in these terms will lead only to an analysis that it is in terminal decline. This is one conclusion which can be drawn, but it is a static view of class which does not suffice in dealing with the working-class in Britain in the 21st century. To do so, we need to be able to develop a theory which can integrate new forms of work organisation, a feminisation of the workforce, a degree of insecurity in paid labour, and the political and organisational forms to which these give rise, while insisting on the centrality of the relationship of exploitation which is at the heart of capitalism. This means also integrating a theory of oppression within Marxist theory.

Marx defined class as a relationship based on how wealth was produced, which in capitalist society is the process of exploitation, involving the extraction of surplus value in the form of profit. Membership of a class is created through that economic relationship, which is an objective one; as Marx put it, it requires only the creation of a class in itself, which exists whether or not members of that class are conscious of their own exploitation. In this he made a distinction between a class which is objectively exploited, and one which is fully class-conscious of that exploitation, as we will see below.[1]

Capitalist society creates two major contending classes, the bourgeoisie and the proletariat, who are defined by their relationship to the means of production. The crucial division here is whether the members of a class control or own the means of production (by definition a small minority but an exceptionally powerful class) or whether, as in the case of most people under capitalism, they find it necessary to sell their labour power in order to cover the costs of their subsistence. There is a fundamental antagonism between these classes because the fruits of the labour of those who sell their labour power are taken from them through the process of exploitation.

This bare bones of Marx's theory should not preclude us from understanding it as a theory which explains far more than the economic relationships directly involved in exploitation. Marx's theory of class was central to his analysis of oppression within capitalist society, since he and Engels connected women's oppression in particular to the rise of class society and private property. He believed that the precondition for ending oppression lay in the overthrow of class society.

It is possible therefore to see his theory of class not in a narrow or reductionist way, as it is sometimes branded, but as developing a universal and emancipatory character, which can inform movements of those campaigning over a wide range of issues in 21st century capitalist society. These include the specific movements against sexual and racial oppression, which have their roots in the great movements of the 1960s. Movements in defence of housing, opposition to environmental degradation, in support of public services such as libraries and parks, can all be better understood as integral to the class analysis which places the relationship of exploitation and the drive for profit at the heart of the capitalist system.

Working people do not just face exploitation

at work from the specific capitalists who own the means of production there; they also have to hand over large parts of their wages to the landlords, the giant supermarket chains, the privatised companies who charge for once-free services. As Marx and Engels wrote in the *Communist Manifesto*, 'No sooner is the exploitation of the labourer by the manufacturer, so far, at an end, and he receives his wages in cash, than he is set upon by the other portions of the bourgeoisie, the landlord, the shopkeeper, the pawnbroker, etc.'[2]

The restructuring of the working-class in Britain over the past decades has created major challenges in developing theories of class. Changes in the labour process have affected consciousness and ideas about class, and about what is meant by work. The rise of women in the workforce coincided with this major restructuring of British capital historically, especially with the decline in manufacturing industry, which accelerated in the 1970s and 1980s just at a time when women were becoming part of the workforce in large numbers.

Women's employment was central to the expansion of certain sectors of work, for example finance and retail in the private sector (two key features of British capitalism), and education and health in the public sector. Women were motivated to work by a series of social and economic factors: the expansion of education, the ability of women to command higher reward for work, the ideological changes in attitudes to women and of women themselves, the decline of marriage and childbirth. Married women entering the labour market in large numbers coincided with the decline of the single male wage, which became increasingly inadequate to maintain higher levels of consumption.[3]

However, as some women's jobs expanded, they also took on characteristics associated more traditionally with manual or routine clerical work. Wages were often pushed down: this was true in areas where women had traditionally been in a small minority but now became the majority workforce, for example in banking or printing industries.[4] White-collar occupations, which might once have been associated with higher status, tended to lose that advantage when they became mass occupations, more subject to the same pressures as traditional working-class jobs. The introduction of machinery into clerical and retail work accelerated this process.

With the development of layers of management in industry, and the possibility of greater supervision, workers were subject to more managerial control and less autonomy as employees. This process, often referred to as proletarianisation, has increased the common characteristics between white-collar and blue-collar work. It has also been a feature of many professional occupations, for example teaching and lecturing, where work is subject to greater control, monitoring, supervision and assessment.[5]

Public services, which employ large numbers of women, have also become subject to these aspects of control. Women increased their participation in the labour market at a time when their conditions worsened alongside many of those of working-class men, as there has been a greater tendency to longer hours, more supervision, intensification of work, and so on. A minority of women have, however, also become part of managerial structures, leading to a small increase in women CEOs and higher executives, but also to a much more significant layer of feminised middle management, particularly noticeable in education, health and other areas of the public sector.

The working-class in Britain in the 21st century is white-collar as well as manual, and is much more diverse. Women's changing role in the workforce and their centrality as white-collar workers means that their class location is important to define. Traditional approaches to class and the nature of the working-class, whether from a Marxist or Weberian point of view, have struggled to analyse the phenomenon of women working outside the home if they fail to acknowledge the changes described above, and if they retain the traditional view of the working-class, as composed largely of male manual workers.[6]

Marx's view of class as a relationship, which hinges on the centrality of exploitation and whether or not an individual has to sell her or his labour power in order to live, allows the definition of the working-class to be extended to different groups who are dependent on work for their livelihood. This leads to a wider and inclusive view of what constitutes the working-class and so help to explain class in the 21st century.[7] It also allows us to place the exploitation of workers and the sale of labour power at the centre of analysis of new forms of work, including work in the digital age.[8]

Adopting a wider definition of class also allows us to include analytically those who are future or past members of the working-class (students or pensioners, for example), those who might work in different sectors of the economy, or in different types of work. It sees class as a fluid and dynamic rather than static concept. The definition that all such people are dependent on the sale of labour power for their subsistence also encompasses within it large sections of the oppressed: most women, LGBT+, Black and ethnic minorities fall within the definition, demonstrating a close connection between class exploitation and specific oppression.

The most recent class survey in Britain, which took place in 2013, takes a very different and more fragmented view of class. Its approach has been to replace the standard method of defining class sociologically with more modern methods that try to take into account a range of cultural and social factors, including self-defini-tion.[9] Similar theoretical approaches have drawn on the writing of Bourdieu to look at different aspects of class in relation to cultural questions in the wider sense.[10]

However, their findings are in sharp con-trast to ones which locate the centrality of work in definition of class; they are updated versions of traditional sociological approaches which stress patterns of consumption or behaviour. *The Great British Class Survey* goes further: there must be serious questions about a study of class which does not even take into account the occu-pation of the person being defined as part of a particular class. Instead the class location of a particular individual is defined by the work locations of those it is acquainted with, and through various social and cultural manifesta-tions including 'cultural capital': the idea that despite a lack of actual capital, certain groups of people may have access to advantages in society because of their education, their knowledge, style of dress or appearance.[11]

While there are important insights here, it tends to reduce class to an individual and subjective question, and in this sense does not differ markedly from traditional sociological theories based on consumption or lifestyles. It is also a self-selecting survey, heavily over-representing professional and managerial groups, while under-representing black and ethnic minorities and those in traditional manual working-class jobs. This in itself may be an indicator of the importance of actual or cultural capital, but it reinforces the view that those who own the actual means of production also control the mental means of production.

This assessment of class also stresses the horizontal fragmentation and separate characteristics of what might be termed the lower classes, or lower-middle and working-class. It therefore assesses particular class locations on the basis of age and cultural habits, which seems an inadequate distinction. Different cultural habits or indeed levels of education between older and younger people are a reality, as are different attitudes, but this can be compatible with those people belonging to the same class. The granddaughter of a car worker or a clerk may obtain a university degree, and develop different attitudes from those of her family, but if she continues to find work in a coffee shop, or a retail outlet, or a call centre, then her relationship to the means of production will be similar to theirs.

In contrast, Marxist views which have stressed a greater tendency towards commonality of class interests and towards the 'proletarianisation' of a number of once professional occupations, allow the possibility of unifying superficially different groups into particular classes. The survey does also, however, point to greater polarisation between the 'elite' and the 'precariat', which demonstrates a recognition of the high levels of inequality within British society, but does not locate this inequality in the process of intensified exploitation.

The need to sell their labour power in order to cover the costs of their reproduction is essential for most women at work. Whatever the extent of the 'family wage' and the idea of the male breadwinner family in the past, they are no longer realities among the vast majority of the working-class, and therefore most women will have a direct relationship to the means of production regardless of their husband's position, or indeed whether they are married. Women face insecure and often difficult conditions at work, as well as the continued major responsibility for childcare and domestic labour, which will be discussed further below.

However, different conditions within the working-class have always existed, and should not be seen as representing different class interests. Those who are unemployed or engaged in full-time domestic labour, for example, should not be seen as outside the working-class, but as sections of it who temporarily or even perhaps permanently are not engaged in wage labour. Guy Standing's 'precariat' should not be seen as cut off from more stable workers, but as a dispossessed section of the working-class with the same interests.[12] His insight into the levels of uncertainty and insecurity among younger workers, well-educated but unable to access permanent, secure and high-status jobs, nor the kind of economic and social security which accompanies such jobs, provides a sharp focus to examine the changing nature of work in Britain.

However, it tends to ignore the fact that such precarity is not the exception for the working-class historically, but very much the rule. Nor does it explain how different work experiences for different generations of the working-class do not negate the nature of exploitation, but suggest the way that an exploitative system can adapt to different expectations on behalf of workers, and the extent to which the amount of surplus value extracted in this process can change. In addition, it suggests that this is the normal condition of exploited young people at work today, whereas the picture is much more uneven.

Notes

1. H Draper, *Karl Marx's Theory of Revolution vol. II: The Politics of Social Classes*, (1978), p. 40-41; Marx and Engels *Collected Works* 6, (1976), p. 211).

2. Marx and Engels, *Selected Works*, (1968), p.42

3. On this see V Beechey, and E Whitelegg, (eds), *Women in Britain Today*, (1986); P Gregg and J Wadsworth, *The*

State of Working Britain, (1999); P Hewitt, *About Time*, (1993); J Rubery, *Women and Recession*, (1988).

4. H Braverman, *Labour and Monopoly Capital*, (1974).

5. K Randle and N Brady, 'Managerialism and Professionalism in the "Cinderella service"' *Journal of Vocational Education and Training* 49,1, (1997), p.121-139

6. S Todd, *The People: The Rise and Fall of the Working-class 1910-2010*, (2014).

7. See Braverman, *Labour and Monopoly Capital*; EO Wright, *The Debate on Classes*, (1989); J Westergaard, *Who gets What?*, (1995).

8. R Crompton, *Class and Stratification*, (1993); U Huws, 'The underpinnings of class in a digital age: living, labour and value', in Panitch et al, *Socialist Register 2014* (2013); J Rubery, *Women and Recession*, (1988).

9. M Savage and F Devine, *The Great British Class Survey*, (2013); M Savage, *Social Class in the 21st Century*, (2015).

10. M Devine, *Rethinking Class*, (2005).

11. P Bourdieu, *The Forms of Capital*, (1986)

12. G Standing, *The Precariat: The New Dangerous Class*, (2011); B Palmer, 'Reconsiderations of Class: precariousness as proletarianisation' in Panitch, *Socialist Register*.

Social reproduction

The existence of large numbers of women in the workforce who are also mothers has created a need to understand women's economic role in production and reproduction within capitalism. There is an ongoing relationship between the work carried out socially in paid employment and the role of unpaid labour within the family (still in large part carried out by women). The relationship between women's role in social production and privatised reproduction under capitalism has been the subject of much debate about the relative positions of women and men inside the working-class, and whether unpaid labour in the household (carried out overwhelmingly by women) can be seen as socially productive, producing value for the capitalist class. The debates also considered whether domestic labour carried out in the home could be considered a mode of production which can be viewed as something distinct from the capitalist mode of production.

The 'domestic labour debate', as it came to be known in the 1970s, entailed recognition of the important economic work carried out in the home, and was an attempt to locate women's domestic labour within the capitalist economy. Some placed the location of women's oppression in the contradiction between their role in social labour and in domestic labour, and the necessity of women having to carry out labour in both spheres of work. Others considered whether the housewife through her labour created some sort of value for the capitalist class, beyond the use values produced within the home. There was also the argument that workers in the home should be considered as part of the labour force, producing value for capital and therefore entitled to recognition and to wages for housework.[1]

The strength of the debate was its attempt to use Marxist categories and concepts of class in order to provide a material basis for women's oppression. However, it was characterised by an analytical separation between the domestic and industrial spheres, and an idealised view of the housewife where there was a decreasing correspondence to reality even in the 1970s. In addition, the danger of simply stating that domestic labour was unproductive labour in only producing use values underplayed its central role to capital and to the reproduction of labour power. This was an insight which the 'wages for housework' theorists understood, even if their political conclusions were widely rejected.

While housework and childcare do not produce commodities, but rather use values within the home, to state this does not adequately locate domestic labour in terms of its importance to capital, nor does it recognise the changes in housework and women's role caused by increasing participation of women in the labour market.

The amount of necessary labour carried out in the home diminishes the amount of wage labour that can be performed by members of the family outside the home, so the drive to commodify domestic tasks in order to free women for greater participation in wage labour has been considerable. Marx foresaw this development: 'Domestic work, such as sewing and mending, must be replaced by the purchase of ready-made articles. Hence, the diminished expenditure of labour in the house is accompanied by an increased expenditure of money outside'.[2]

Labour once carried out in the home is now often replaced by services bought on the market or commodities which aid or substitute for use values once produced in the home. In the middle-class family, there has been a major rise in employment of paid workers to carry out a range of tasks from cleaning, cooking, gardening and childcare. In the working-class family those tasks are still carried out by unpaid labour of the family members (with the partial exception of childcare, although for low-paid working-class women this still relies heavily on informal arrangements with family or friends).

The emphasis in the family today is more on its role as a centre for the reproduction of labour power, especially renewed generations of labour power, an essential need for capital. Women's labour in the home, as well as producing use values, also contributes to the reproduction of labour power, and therefore *indirectly* contributes to the production of surplus value. If not directly productive of surplus value, it was nonetheless essential to the continued production of that surplus value.

This is a similar approach to much materialist feminism where a number of critiques have stressed that any theory of oppression had to be based in social relationships, to have a historical view and to consider the gender division of labour as central.[3] Lise Vogel rejects dual systems theory and stresses the centrality of the reproduction of labour power to capital, and the role of this reproduction as central to the oppression of women. Domestic labour for social reproduction is at the heart of the refreshing of labour power, which is essential to capitalist production.[4] Vogel argues that women play a key role in social reproduction because of their specific and unique role in childbirth and lactation. She considers that it is the process of social reproduction itself, rather than the family form, which is its most important aspect, and that in this sense women's role in social reproduction leads to their oppression.[5]

While Vogel makes a clear and compelling case for the centrality to capitalism of social reproduction, this takes a somewhat abstract view of how labour power is reproduced. She poses alternatives to the family for example, that a labour force can be replenished through immigration or slavery. However, this still involves labour power being reproduced in a family, but in a family that can take various forms geographically and historically.

In addition, it can be argued that institutions such as prisons or care homes, which carry out some of the same functions of the family, are not serious rivals to the nuclear family, which is the overwhelming site of reproduction of labour power. Even considering the commodification of some family functions, and women working outside the home over past thirty years, the family has if anything been enhanced as a site for the reproduction of labour power not diminished. It could be argued that capitalism has in some ways strengthened the family by making it more accommodating to diversity, for example with gay marriage. Nonetheless, social reproduction theory as outlined by Vogel has the strength of locating women's oppression in the needs of capital and thus relating it to class theory.

Any theory of class has to be able to integrate the role of social reproduction into its analysis. It otherwise ignores women's central role in ensuring the next generation of workers is cared for, socialised, educated, and kept healthy in order to be fit to perform its function of producing the surplus value which leads to the accumulation of capital. The fact that this task is still carried out within and around the family at relatively little cost to the capitalist class, in addition to the role in paid employment now carried out by millions of women (nearly half the workforce in the UK is composed of women), heightens the very close relationship which we can now discern between women's employment in social production and their lack of paid employment in social reproduction.

Notes

1. For a selection of these debates see M Benston, 'The Political Economy of Women's Liberation', *Monthly Review* 21,4 (1969); J Harrison, 'The political economy of housework', *Bulletin of the Conference of Socialist Economists* 4 (1974); M DallaCosta and S James, *The Power of Women and the Subversion of the Community*, (1975); S Federici, 'Wages against Housework' reprinted in E Malos, *The Politics of Housework* (1980); J Gardiner et al, 'Women's Domestic Labour', *Conference of Socialist Economists* (1976); W Seccombe, 'The housewife and her labour under capitalism' *New Left Review* 83, (1974); J Smith, 'Women and the Family', *International Socialism* 100, (1978). For my contemporary analysis see L German, *Sex, Class and Socialism*, (1989).

2. Marx, *Capital*, vol I, (1976), p. 518

3. I Young, 'Socialist Feminism and the Limits of Dual Systems Theory', reprinted in R Hennessy and C Ingraham, *Materialist Feminism*, (1997).

4. M Giminez and L Vogel, (eds), *Science and Society* 69, 1, (2005).

5. L Vogel, *Marxism and the Oppression of Women*, (1983).

Class consciousness

Marx and Engels recognised both the unevenness of consciousness within society on the one hand, and the transformative power of capitalism on the other, which acted to destroy or weaken old social divisions and structures. This exploitative and oppressive system of private property and the accumulation of profit means that transformation of the system can only take place collectively, on the part of those who produce the wealth. In that process the exploited class would experience a transformation of consciousness, which would rid them of 'the muck of ages' as Marx described it.[1] In other words, women and men would, in the process of making the revolution, develop a consciousness which overcame the divisions within the working-class on grounds of sexism, racism or nationality.

Marxism is a theory whose ontological aspects are closely connected to its epistemology, or theory of knowledge. Marx's view of what constitutes 'species being', the ability to consciously labour, his theory of alienation in which this capacity is lost as a result of the operation of wage labour under capitalism, and his theory of how workers are both able to recognise and overcome this loss, are themselves a closely bound, mediated totality. In Marx there is no reductive relationship between being and consciousness, but neither is there a false opposition between what it is to be human, the loss of control over this condition, the intellectual and ideological appreciation of this fact, and the struggle to overcome this condition.

Marx saw ideas as developing from (changing) material reality and sometimes altering sharply as a result of changing circumstances: 'Life is not determined by consciousness, but consciousness by life'.[2] Marxist theory is concerned with the connection between objective factors in society and the subjective role of actors which can lead to certain outcomes, a point he made famously in his comment, 'Men make their own history, but not of their own free will; not under circumstances they themselves have chosen but under the given and inherited circumstances with which they are directly confronted'.[3]

Marx's thought was influenced by the rational and scientific ideas of the eighteenth-century Enlightenment, but he built on, and provided a critique of, these ideas to develop a dialectical theory of change in history which stressed the contradictions in society. A major criticism of Marxism is that it is too deterministic, stressing the inevitability of change and the certainty of progress towards socialism.[4] This would be a more accurate criticism of certain forms of Enlightenment materialism, but it is a one-sided reading of Marx's theory. There have been major debates within both classical and more modern Marxism over the relationship between the subjective and objective circumstances, or over structure and agency; both these discussions are concerned with the role of individual actors in particular given circumstances.[5]

The central argument hinges on whether progress towards social change is inevitable or whether it is dependent on the actions of men and women; and this notion of a previously determined teleological economic progress to socialism marked much Marxist and other socialist theory.[6] Its fundamental weakness was its prognosis of inevitability which missed out questions of contingency and agency. This reliance on development of economic structures as automatically bringing social progress was challenged by Marxist historians such as De St Croix and Thompson, who tried to develop Marx's ideas to consider class as a relationship, and the working-class as both the subject and object of history.[7]

In doing so they considered class both from an economic point of view, but also from the question of class consciousness, in other words what made people think of themselves as being part of a certain class. Such analyses attempted to go beyond the immediate manifestations of social and class differences to examine the underlying relationships at the centre of any class society. It is perhaps not accidental that the late 1960s and early 1970s saw a revival in interest of Marxists such as the Hungarian Georg Lukács and the Italian Antonio Gramsci. Both dealt with questions of consciousness and possibilities of revolution. The widespread interest in these theories on the left and in academia in the 1970s brought a new series of insights into this debate, especially Gramsci's concept of the need to fight for hegemony for Marxist ideas within capitalist society.[8]

Notes

1. Marx and Engels, *The German Ideology* (1965), p. 86

2. Ibid., p.38

3. Marx, *Surveys from Exile*, p.146

4. For a recent critique see P Paolucci, *Marx's Scientific Dialectics: A Methodological Treatise for a New Century*, (2009).

5.   For some of the classic works on these debates see F
     Jakubowski, *Ideology and Superstructure in Historical
     Materialism*, (1978); G Lukács, *History and Class
     Consciousness* (1971); R Luxemburg, *Selected Political
     Writings*, (1971). For more recent commentary, see A
     Callinicos, *Making History*, (1987).

6.   See on this M Salvadori, *Karl Kautsky and the Socialist
     Revolution 1880-1988*, (1979), p.115-180; J Rees, *The
     Algebra of Revolution*, (1998), p.126-169.

7.   G De St Croix, *The Class Struggle in the Ancient Greek
     World*, (1981); EP Thompson, *The Making of the English
     Working-class* (1968).

8.   Marx and Engels, *The German Ideology* (1965), p. 86

How the political and ideological relate to the economic

For those on the left in Britain, many of whose older adherents were politicised and developed from the late 1960s onwards, especially during the great industrial battles of the first half of the 1970s, working-class consciousness and advance are inextricably connected with objective measurements such as strike days 'lost', number of strikes, and level of union organisation. There are obviously extremely sound reasons for judging levels of struggle by these criteria, since they measure the extent to which workers are prepared to take concrete industrial action in pursuit of their demands. It must be added that no major challenge to capitalist power which wants to achieve permanent change can do so without putting trade-union organisation and particularly generalised strike action at its centre. Rosa Luxemburg wrote that, 'Where the chains of capitalism are forged, there they must be broken'.[1]

However, the converse is not necessarily true: low levels of strike action do not automatically suggest lack of political awareness or even lack of class consciousness. It is clear that the British trade-union movement entered a very long dark night with the major defeats of the 1980s, especially those of the miners and print workers, a night from which it has not totally emerged. This, the punitive nature of the trade-union laws, which impose legal and financial penalties on any serious solidarity action, and the effects of privatisation and deindustrialisation, all took their toll. The unions' historic closeness to the peculiarly British form of reformism known as Labourism has also often meant a political weakness at the head of the unions, and a reluctance to engage in the forms of militant action which could have defeated such attacks.

However, the weakening of trade-union organisation and overt class struggle has meant that levels of political consciousness re-emerged in different ways: through the Labour landslide in the election of 1997 which heralded 13 years of Labour government; and through high levels of political consciousness on issues including war. The demonstration in February 2003 against the Iraq war remains the largest ever in British history, involving all the major trade-unions, very large sections of the Muslim community and other Black and minority ethnic groups, large numbers of women, and sections of the middle classes. It was the expression of a very high degree of consciousness around the issue, and the related one of Palestine, which continues to have its effect. Anti-war consciousness today remains high in Britain, an important factor in a country with such an imperialist hinterland, and which plays such a major role in supporting US foreign policy.

While political support for the main party

of working people has declined from its hey-day in the years after the Second World War, increases in support for various movements including against austerity, have grown. Large numbers of people in Britain, including many young people, identify as being on the left, including between one and two million who see themselves as 'far left'. This has increased since the 1980s.[2] Sizeable minorities of people, including many workers, volunteer that they have taken part in some sort of do-it-yourself political activity, for example, demonstrating, signing a petition, boycotting or engaging in some other form of protest.[3]

It is therefore misleading to read a lack of political interest from the lack of industrial and economic struggle. Nor should this over-all decline obscure the high levels of political consciousness, nor the contested but sizeable levels of support for the industrial action which does take place. Indeed, one of the features of British society in the 21st century is a level of awareness among a sizeable minority, includ-ing among trade-unionists, about many of the problems and difficulties with the system, an awareness of questions of oppression, and a willingness to challenge the status quo.

This political consciousness is much less likely to be located within traditional parties (with the partial exception of Corbyn's Labour). It also for the most part is not informed by -although it may be sympathetic to the general ideas of - ideological Marxism. The involvement of this layer of people in wider movements does however give Marxists the possibility of relating to them and putting forward ideological answers to the questions thrown up by them.

Notes

1. Luxemburg, *Selected Political Writings*, p.397

2. A Cousins, 'The crisis of the British regime', http://www.counterfire.org/theory/37-theory/14906-the-crisis-of-the-british-regime-democracy-protest-and-the-unions#left (Accessed 20.6.16)

3. Cousins, 'Crisis'. Pippa Norris shows patterns of political activity around protest increasing in western Europe and the US in the late 20th century, alongside a decline in likelihood to vote by young people. P Norris, *Democratic Phoenix*, (2002), p.195, pp.197-8.

The employers' offensive and the state of working-class organisation in Britain today

The opening section on work highlighted the decline of trade-union organisation under the impact of 35 years of offensive by successive governments and employers, going alongside structural changes which devastated many highly unionised sectors, while seeing jobs increasing in very weakly organised sectors such as finance, retail and catering. The cumulative effect has been felt in terms of what would be described in Marxist terms as an increase in the rate of exploitation. This has been achieved through the slimming down of jobs, often through privatisation, the cutting of rest and lunch breaks, the increase in various forms of flexibility which leads to multi-tasking, the increase in working hours through having to commute further, the lengthening of working hours and cutting of overtime pay, the increase in supervision, surveillance and targets for performance, and increasingly the reduction in real wages.

These features have been exacerbated by the banking crash and recession of 2008. Wages have fallen in real terms since then, leading to a real reduction in working-class incomes and a major growth in inequality. This wage loss has particularly affected the young, who also suffer high levels of unemployment.[1] Levels of inequality have grown, with those in the capital some of the worst. The poverty rate in London stood at 28% in 2011.[2] The Greater London Authority announced in 2008 that as a rule of thumb, life expectancy falls by one year for each stop that is travelled eastwards on the Jubilee Line from Westminster, from the richest part of the city to the much poorer parts in the south and east.[3]

The recession has worsened inequality by a combination of measures. A workplace survey carried out in 2011 found that British companies had responded to the recession in a variety of ways, most commonly by freezing wages, which had been carried out by 41% of those questioned and by a major 64% in the public sector, freezing the filling of vacant posts (28%) and changing organisation of work (25%). Again, incidence of these was considerably higher in the public sector.[4] In the same survey, employees reported the most common effect of the recession as more work and less pay. More than a third of public-sector employees reported an increase in workload. Some of the worst hit industries included construction and public administration for wage freezes, and increases in workload in public administration, transport and communication and financial services.[5]

Wage freezes and cuts have been accompanied by cuts to paid holidays and reductions in employers' pension contributions. Use of zero-hours contracts, while still covering a relatively small number of workers, doubled in these companies between 2004 and 2011, and increased in larger companies. There was also an increase in shift working.[6] While small and powerful groups such as London tube workers have maintained and even increased their living standards, others such as university lecturers have seen wages driven down by 14% since the financial crisis and an increase in exploitation through the undercutting of conditions, casualisation, and performance targets.[7]

Employers remain resistant to change for the most part, refusing to share more of their profits, driving down pensions, and finding ways of evading statutory wage increases. The recent establishment of a fairly pitiful living-wage level by the government has been honoured in the breach as employers have implemented it while cutting other aspects of wages, for example by cutting extra payments for weekend work, leaving workers sometimes even worse off than before the original wage increase! The compensation for these low wages is an encouragement of historically high levels of personal debt, and the active fostering by government of a bubble in housing prices which is resulting in great misery for many working-class people.

If Britain is rapidly becoming a low-wage economy, it is also increasingly a low-productivity one. It is estimated that French workers could take every Friday off and still be as productive as British workers working a five-day week.[8] This low productivity is a particular problem for Britain; it reflects the other side of the low-wage economy, that it is cheaper to employ workers on low wages than to invest in machinery and new technology.

The Bleak House of British workplace relations shows no sign of being changed from above. While there appears to be growing disquiet even among ruling-class circles about the consequences of neoliberal policies and the growing discontent around them, there is no plan B. Indeed, a whole series of seemingly inexorable forces continue on their pre-ordained path: EU decrees and regulations, the pressures of international competition both in Europe and beyond, the path set for public services such as the NHS and higher education, which are increasingly being opened up to competition, or in other words are being forced to compete externally and internally with privatised competitors.

Trade-union organisation is weak in the private sector, with majority union membership in only 3% of private-sector workplaces.[9] Even in private-sector workplaces where unions are recognised, nearly half reported in 2011 that there was no bargaining over pay. In many parts of the public sector, pay bargaining at a national level has been dramatically weakened.[10]

The British ruling class has succeeded in shifting the share of wealth going to employers, and decreasing that going to the working-class, both in terms of direct wages and in terms of a wider 'social wage'. Even major and highly profitable companies force some or all of their workforces onto zero-hours contracts, and demand increased flexibility in terms of when and where their employees work. In the driving down of wages and conditions, workers in once relatively well-rewarded public-sector jobs find that the process of privatisation and the opening up to competition increases their rate of exploitation; in private-sector enterprises the same process is under way, with the most rapacious and anti-worker policies forcing the pace.

There are sometimes political scandals over

these issues, but there is little legal or other
restraint over the companies concerned. Sports
Direct is the most notorious, where a sports
clothing and equipment warehouse has been
set up in a former mining village, employ-
ing very largely migrant labour from Eastern
Europe, paying what is effectively below the
minimum wage, searching workers (unpaid) at
the end of their shifts, deducting pay for 'trans-
gressions', and creating such conditions that
there are reports of pregnant women giving
birth in the toilets. These conditions are remi-
niscent of the conditions of the working-class
during the Industrial Revolution 200 years ago.

Unite the union is involved in a major campaign to unionise which includes providing
free English lessons for potential members.[11]
Recent threatened or real closures of established companies, such as Tata Steel or the
retailer BHS, have provoked opposition not just
because of the major job losses involved but
because their pension-fund deficits (which are
after all only deferred wages) have apparently
not prevented dividend payments to sharehold-
ers or directors before the companies failed.

Discontents among British workers about their situation at are not hard to find: with support for groups of workers who do take action, with a refusal to accept some of the worst conditions which is leading groups of workers in different sectors to strike action (most notably the junior doctors), with growing discontent over relentless austerity, leading to many local campaigns and big national demonstrations, with a movement over housing which is in acute crisis. The different campaigns and movements, however, lack the national coordination necessary to bring them to successful outcomes, and this is not provided by the TUC, the major umbrella for most trade-unions, which has not distinguished itself by either clarity or boldness in opposing the attacks. The response of individual trade-union leaderships has been much more variable, but has resulted for the most part in little strike action although sometimes a high level of political campaigning.

While the combination of highly restrictive trade-union laws (solidarity strike action is illegal in the UK), the closeness of many trade-union leaders to the Labour apparatus, and

the tendency towards quietism and passivity
from those trade-union leaders, has led to the
very low level of strikes in total numbers, in
addition to the very low level of strikes lasting
longer than one or two days, political discontent with governments and with neoliberalism
more widely has led to a considerable degree
of political campaigning initiated or supported
by sections of the trade-union bureaucracy.

The Communication Workers' Union, com-
prised of largely manual post and telecoms
workers, has been involved in the People's
Assembly, the radical anti-austerity movement. It has also created its own mass events
called the People's Post, campaigning against
the industry's privatisation. The leadership
was able to get Jeremy Corbyn, newly elected
as Labour leader, to speak at a mass rally in
Manchester Cathedral when the Tory party conference was taking place in the city in October
2015. The union also hosted a mass Jeremy
Corbyn for PM event at its annual conference
where nearly 3,000 people attended.

The civil-service union PCS and Labour-
affiliated Unite have also been at the centre of

supporting non-union grassroots initiatives such as the People's Assembly, the convoy to Calais to take aid to refugees, and the anti-war movement. Unite and the GMB have also set up branches for members of the community who may not be in paid work. These initiatives have been very important in developing a wider political and activist consciousness, and of linking the unions with the movements need outside the workplace.

While any consideration of strike figures and union organisation would reveal a substantial weakness within the British working-class, they do not take into account a wider radicalisation, strong among the young but also among older workers who were strongly anti-war and anti-austerity. It is arguable that some of these initiatives have helped staunch the decline of many unions, and in some cases reversed this decline. They also contributed to the election of Jeremy Corbyn, to which we will return below.

Notes

1. D Blanchflower and S Machin, 'Falling real wages',
    Centrepiece (2014), http://cep.lse.ac.uk/pubs/download/
    cp422.pdf (Accessed 20.6.16)

2. T MacInnes et al, *London's Poverty Profile*, (2011), p.7

3. Greater London Authority Information, (2008), p.77

4. Van Waanroy et al, *The 2011 Workplace Employment
    Relations Study First Findings*, (2011), p.7

5. Ibid., p.8

6. Ibid., p. 10

7. http://www.theguardian.com/education/2016/
    may/25/uk-university-lecturers-strike-over-pay
    (Accessed 20.6.16)

8. http://www.ft.com/cms/s/0/c413ca76-ce3c-11e4-86fc-
    00144feab7de.html#axzz4BXypfmbJ

9. Van Wanrooy, *2011 Workplace Employment Relations*, p. 14

10. Ibid., p.22

11. http://www.unitetheunion.org/campaigning/
    support-sports-direct-workers---sign-our-petition/

Two souls
of Labourism

There are many differences between the US Democratic Party candidate Bernie Sanders and Jeremy Corbyn, both in the context of their recent high-profile campaigns and in the particular policies that they espouse. I would argue that Corbyn's record on opposing foreign-policy decisions and imperialist expansion is much stronger than that of Sanders, but there is little question that they both speak for voices which have been increasingly both radicalised and disenfranchised in recent years, and which have been left without a political voice as a result of the move of politicians to the 'extreme centre'.[1]

These voices include the old trade-union and political left politicised by 1968 and its aftermath, the young radicalised by a series of events and issues from war to climate change, the Muslim communities increasingly under the cosh of institutional racism of which they are now the main target, those individuals who have found themselves victims of various aspects of neoliberal policies, including zero-hours contracts, rocketing rents and house prices, student tuition fees, and the wholesale theft of once-promised pensions which they now have to pay for.

The scale of Corbyn's win was a surprise to most; his successful candidacy a surprise to everyone, including him. It reflected personal qualities, including tenacity in supporting campaigns, a commitment to sometimes unpopular causes such as Ireland or Palestine, a genuine interest in the people and society around him. His age, like Sanders, also denotes a long-term and principled commitment to socialist politics.

But none of this alone would be enough. What the Corbyn win represented was a reflection of the mass movements of the left which have been central to British politics for over 15 years. These include trade-union organised demonstrations and those organised by students, grassroots anti-austerity movements, Occupy, the anti-war and Palestine movements and many more. The movements themselves and their importance is partly a reflection of the low level of class struggle but also of a growing and greater politicisation on the left. There have been attempts to construct new parties of the left out of some of these movements, better able to reflect the aspirations of the left than New Labour. The most successful of these was Respect, but for a number of reasons it did not achieve sufficient breakthrough.[2]

This led to the strange situation whereby the radical voices so critical of all the main bourgeois parties in British and looking for a left alternative found their expression in the Corbyn campaign. The scale of support and its enthusiasm galvanised the left but terrified many of Corbyn's colleagues in the Parliamentary Labour Party. They regard his policies as anathema and have subjected him to appalling public attack and are doing all they can to ensure their prophecies of his un-electability are fulfilled. The MPs express various contradictions within Labour: between its base and more right-wing representatives; between anti-war and anti-austerity policies held by many Labour members and voters and the much more right-wing views of most MPs; between the demands of the radical movement and the triangulation which has pulled Labour to the right under Blair and subsequently.

Labour was created by the trade-unions as their representative in parliament and its make-up still reflects that influence. In addition, Labour has always been in support of empire (the Attlee government post 1945 had a poor record on its attitude to decolonisation and national-liberation movements), and in many cases adopted a consensus foreign-policy with the Tories.[3] A Corbyn victory has caused turmoil in this area, with bitter divisions between him and his right-wing critics over issues ranging from war in Syria, the renewal of the Trident nuclear submarine system, and the question of Palestine.

The debates over these issues have seen Labour MPs cheered by their Tory opponents in an attempt to isolate and defeat Corbyn. Foreign policy issues are also on the agenda with the recent publication of the Chilcot report into the Iraq war, which was highly critical of Tony Blair and his allies. The tensions between Corbyn and his MPs can be expected to grow in these areas.

The problem facing Corbyn is the contradiction between his mass base of support and the nature of the PLP and the Labour apparatus. While he has much more support among the trade-union bureaucracy (at least partly because of the attitudes of many of their members towards him), they too have a great deal of weight and have historically helped to reinforce the right within Labour. The reforms in voting for leader introduced by Corbyn's predecessor, Ed Miliband, weakened their voting powers in elections, as it did that of the MPs, but they still exercise considerable influence.[4]

One reason for the virulence of the attacks on Corbyn from Labour's right, from the Tory government and from the vast majority of the media is that - contrary to their claims - he is actually relatively well placed to head the next government. While this is scheduled for 2020, there are signs that it could come earlier, especially given the uncertainties of the referendum over EU and the civil war now being waged within the governing party. The unpopularity of the government and the fragmentation of British politics could well allow a Labour government or Labour-led coalition to take office. Fear of this explains the constant attacks, the attempts to blame him for every political eventuality and the regular briefings to the press about the latest new challenger to him, as the right do everything that they can to depose him before he has the chance to win an election.

Such an eventuality is still a way off, and there are many barriers to his success. As importantly, there is enough historical precedent to demonstrate that winning such elections is only the first hurdle. A left British prime minister would face challenges from within his own party and those around it; from big business; from the capitalist state;

and from the international institutions ranging from the EU to the IMF and Nato who act in the collective interests of neoliberal capital.

Any left government would need to take strong measures to defend itself against these attacks, to challenge the power of major unelected institutions, and to deliver reforms for the people who elected it. Such measures could succeed without challenging the power of capital and without a movement based in the working-class which could act independently of the government to secure its demands. It is impossible to say what will happen to Jeremy Corbyn in the future because there are too many unknowns and too many intangibles.

A fundamental for socialists is that a left leader could be in office but not in power. However, the majority of the left in Britain has welcomed Corbyn's victory, seeing it as an endorsement of the sorts of policies we have been fighting for over many years. At the very least, it has created an audience for and a discussion about left politics which can only strengthen the left if it takes advantage of the opportunities it presents.

Notes

1. T Ali, *The Extreme Centre: A Warning*, (2015). The phrase was coined by socialist campaigner Tariq Ali to describe the neoliberal 'centre ground' which has absorbed so many of the representatives of mainstream parties.

2. I was centrally involved in the Respect project and feel that it made a major breakthrough into sections of the working-class looking for an alternative to war and neoliberalism. It received strong support from some Muslim communities, very important in itself in such a racist country, but did so in part because it recognised the class interests of the vast majority of Muslims, something often not recognised on the left. It appealed not just to Muslims, but also to sections of non-Muslim trade-unionists, ex-Labour voters and young people. Its split and subsequent demise after 2007 was a step backward for the left which I regret. A decent account of its strengths and weaknesses remains to be written.

3. J Saville, *The Politics of Continuity: British Foreign Policy and the Labour Government, 1945-46*, (1993).

4. http://www.theguardian.com/politics/blog/2014/mar/01/labour-votes-on-membershipunion-reforms-at-special-conference-politics-live-blog (Accessed 20.6.16)

Prospects for revolutionaries today

In many ways, British society is undergoing a sense of profound change. The post-war certainties on which the welfare state was built are under the most systematic attack, leading to a major crisis in the health service, housing, political governance, institutions.[1] The long-term decline of the two main parties has reached an acute stage. The Tories' bitter divisions over Europe reflect an inability for British capitalism to maintain its old place in the world, and an equal inability to find a successful new role. The crisis over the EU is ripping traditional politics apart, and having an increasing impact on Labour, many of whose voters appear to have rejected the leadership's call for a vote to remain in the EU.

This has now opened up a huge crisis whose outcome is impossible at present to predict. The election of Corbyn demonstrates a desire by many traditional Labour supporters, and many young people, to put the years of Blairism behind them and to create a party based on much more egalitarian and anti-capitalist ideals. Yet it has also revealed the deep problems for Labour, with its inability to deal with the problems of many of its traditional strongholds. Scotland has already abandoned Labour, and there are signs that the old industrial towns and villages, based on industries like mining and steel, are also seeing a weakening of Labour's (mostly right-wing) local base. The picture in London and other big cities is rather different, since Labour is more able to pull together a coalition of different elements of the working-class and left, including migrant communities and young people.

However, the consensus politics of the two main parties over recent decades, the unpopularity of many neoliberal policies, and the impact of the financial crisis since 2008, have all led to a polarisation of British politics to right and left. This has seen support for the two main parties fall electorally. Labour has rebuilt a large membership thanks to Corbyn, but the Tories' membership continues to decline and is ageing. At the same time the nationalists in Scotland have grown on the basis of taking Labour votes by putting forward policies which are clearly social democratic and to Labour's left, although this is less the case in Wales. The Greens picked up a million votes in the 2015 election, while the far-right UKIP scored over 3 million.

This polarisation is a phenomenon across Europe and the US, as we see the growth of far-right politics, but also those of a left anti-austerity variety. The electoral system in Britain, however, still massively favours the main parties since it is based on 'first past the post' which means very unequal distribution of votes. In a way, this is contributing to the present political crisis, since there is often little or no political expression for ideas which are held by considerable numbers of people.

This polarisation has to be set against the historic weakness of the left in Britain. Up until the 1960s and 70s, Labour's (and indeed the Tories') local roots were substantial with high levels of loyalty and commitment from party members and voters, with local structures and offices, and with very close ties to the major manual working-class unions who were the mainstay of Labour. This has not disappeared but weakened, with much higher levels of atomisation and disconnection from working-class communities, and much less ability to determine the politics or even the voting intentions of many workers. The decline of this Labour organisation has also meant a decline of the left in many areas, which was traditionally rooted in the Labour Party. The Communist Party historically has played an important industrial and sometimes intellectual role in influencing the Labour left and wider movement, but it was never a mass party and is now small.

The anti-Stalinist left which emerged from 1968 and the early 1970s still exists, but is weak and often stuck in a time warp which makes it hard to relate to new movements or people. It has neither succeeded in building an electoral alternative to the left of Labour, nor of building mass revolutionary parties on the Leninist model. Part of the problem here has been the strength of Labourism electorally, despite its decline, much of it channelled through trade-union organisation. But there are major issues about the relevance of the left to the concerns and struggles of a working-class which is less organised collectively, more atomised and removed from traditional forms of class consciousness and organisation.

The weakening of British capitalism, the move to the left of Labour, the growing radicalisation among many young people, and the spectre of racism, which is also growing as a result of austerity and crisis, all make it imperative that such a situation cannot be allowed to continue. How then to overcome the major gap between the radical left, its analysis and awareness of the nature of capitalism and the need to overthrow it, and its relative isolation from the mass of working-class people?

It is unlikely to be through the arithmetical

growth provided by small groups combining. Rather, new organisations have to evolve organically from real struggle which alters the relationship between different groups of socialists. That process has to start with a commitment from socialists to engage in active politics (an obvious point but by no means universally adopted on the left). Rosa Luxembourg's epithet 'in the beginning was the deed' demands of socialists that they organise in the most effective way around the issues of the day - whether over racism, war or austerity.[2]

The real experience of activity, and the concrete issues around which working people organise, are the core of socialist organisation, insisting as they do that there can be no theory without practice. It is in these struggles that the demands and theoretical directions of the movement develop. Such activities do not start with decrees from socialists but from the needs of the struggle.

That socialists should engage in activity not on their own but with others should also be obvious, and it is here important to insist on the centrality of Trotsky's theory of the united front.[3] The best of the radical left in Britain has seen this as a critical way of engaging in joint work and therefore political discussion with much larger forces engaged in reformist organisations and politics. The method has been, and continues to be, of central importance in the anti-war and anti-austerity movements. It continues to be relevant in the era of Corbyn's Labour party and of groups such as the left-wing Momentum, which bases itself upon the campaigning activists who worked so hard during his election for leadership.

It is unity around specifics by those from different parties with a commitment to defeating racism, fascism, austerity and war within the united front which allows socialists not only to put forward their ideas and concrete proposals, but to be part of a wider movement and therefore to be able to talk to workers who might not otherwise be attracted to their ideas. In the process of so doing they can help take the movement forward while hopefully also building socialist ideas within it.

The final issue facing socialists in Britain is the construction of a left socialist alternative.

Whatever our hopes for Corbyn, many of us do not see a Labour Party wedded to parliamentary change as being the vehicle to bring about the thoroughgoing transformation of society towards socialism that we need. At the same time, the particular model of the Leninist party developed in Britain post-1968 is showing many signs of wear and tear, not least in its inability to connect with wider groups of workers.

We need a Leninism for the 21st century, one which does not fetishise particular organisational forms but which stands by the principles of democratic socialism, of production for need under workers' control; which bases its ideas on those of the Marxists who developed socialist theory in the 19th and early 20th centuries; which attempts to integrate a theory of oppression into its critique of capitalism; and which has something to say about actually existing capitalism in Britain and internationally in the 21st century.

At the centre of this new Leninism, if it is to succeed, there has to be an openness to new forms of organising and to the principle and method of the united front. That means a profound and ongoing commitment to the movements which arise in and around the working-class movement, and a recognition of putting forward both demands and forms of practice which can unify sections of the working-class, and which have to go beyond the membership of one or the other groups (and indeed beyond membership of the Labour Party, too many of whose left see working-class activity and advance as synonymous with Labour activity and advance). At the same time, the most committed and aware core of those movements needs to be grouped together into political organisation, which connects with the past and the history and theory of the movement, which creates a collective means of solidarity and support for its members, and which develops strategy and tactics in order to take the movement forward.

The idea of Leninism, which was revived in the late 1960s with the post-Stalinist and Trotskyist left, has taken some serious knocks in the past quarter century, most obviously with the fall of the Berlin wall and its aftermath, but also with the growth of horizontalist ideas. There is a need to constantly assess what is changing in the world, including new sorts of organisational and theoretical developments. But the need to build socialist organisation is not an option for the left; it is an essential if the working-class is to move forward.[4]

Notes

1. For an eloquent background to the changes in some major British institutions and the lack of confidence in them see A Sampson, *Who Runs This Place?*, (2004)

2. R Luxemburg, 'Organisational Questions of Russian Social Democracy', P Hudis and KB Anderson (eds), *Rosa Luxemburg Reader*, (2004), p.255

3. L Trotsky, 'On the United Front' https://www.marx-ists.org/archive/trotsky/1924/ffyci-2/08.htm; 'The Question of the United Front' https://www.marxists.org/archive/trotsky/1922/02/uf.htm (Accessed 20.6.16)

4. There have been a number of interesting writings on why such organization is still relevant. Paul Le Blanc is always worth reading, and especially P LeBlanc, *Unfinished Leninism*, (2014). See also J Dean, *Crowds and Party*, (2016) for a critique of movements which deny the need for ongoing collective organization; C Nineham, *Capitalism and Class Consciousness: The ideas of Georg Lukács*, (2010).

Help us remake socialist politics for the 21st century

Counterfire builds the movements against war, austerity, racism and climate change.

Corbyn's victory has helped the left and we need to stay mobilised to support him. We think fundamental change comes from below, and that socialists need to get organised to help make this happen. We want to see a left that can make a real difference to the world and we are growing.

Counterfire.org is one of the best-read websites on the radical left, and we are now producing a regular free tabloid in the same spirit. We have Counterfire groups across the country and they need your help and ideas to make change happen.

Help us remake socialist politics for the twenty-first century. Join us, we are stronger together.

www.counterfire.org/join